Teaching Outside the Curriculum

Vito Michienzi

Published by eVw Press, 2020.

While every precaution has been taken in the preparation of this book, the publisher assumes no responsibility for errors or omissions, or for damages resulting from the use of the information contained herein.

TEACHING OUTSIDE THE CURRICULUM

First edition. October 28, 2020.

Copyright © 2020 Vito Michienzi.

ISBN: 978-1989159088

Written by Vito Michienzi.

Table of Contents

Preface 1
Genesis 3
What Master Teachers Know 5
On the Cult of EduCelebrities 8
Building Rapport the Magician Way 11
Lesson 1: The Audience Doesn't Care 12
Lesson 2: Consider the Needs of Your Audience 15
Lesson 3: You Never Stop Thinking and Practicing 18
Lesson 4: Find Your Voice 21
Lesson 5: Don't Relate, Connect 23
Lesson 6: Authenticity 26
Lesson 7: Be Willing to Stretch 29
Interlude: The Swiss Army Knife vs. The Toolbox 33
Listen and Respond 35
You Can't Fake Authenticity 41
Closing the Door 44
Connect With Every Student 48
Outside the Classroom Counts 51
Keep the Professional Lines Clear 53
Stop Taking Yourself So Seriously 56
When Rapport Fails 58
You Still Need to Teach 60
How Do I Fit it All In? 61
Conclusion 64
Acknowledgements 67

Dedicated to all the teachers who saw the best in every student, even when they refused to let you do so...

And to all those students who wished they had a teacher that could see the best in them.

Preface

This is the third time I've written this preface.

The first time through felt more like an apology as I didn't feel confident about the manuscript—its value to a teacher or its evergreen practicality for the teaching field. Although my first reader (the effervescent Christopher Poulsen) loved it and made many comments on its necessity, my feeling of imposter syndrome caused me to throw it in the drawer while I mulled it over.

The second time was after having one of *those* years in teaching... the one where classes are wild, home life is chaotic and your personal life was holding on by a thread. I honestly felt like a failure by the end, but then a student anonymously sent this to my school board:

"This teacher is certainly the best teacher I've ever had and has changed who I am for the better. He strives to make the learning environment a safe and positive place, and makes learning, well, really fun. He doesn't ever give up on anyone and always puts in his best effort with all of his students to teach them."

First, I was in tears because it was too much for me to handle. It meant more to me than any encouragement from a colleague or friend ever could. Then I realized if I could get *that* kind of response after having *that* kind of year, maybe I was doing something right. Still, I wasn't feeling confident about this manuscript.

And now, it's being written in the most unprecedented time of the past hundred years. In one year, we've had a teacher strike, followed by a global pandemic, resulting in the classroom being closed and teachers scrambling to retool their teaching.

It's time to release this book.

Why?

The one thing made clear, that even with the multitude of pedagogies, tools and professional development given to the profession over the years, was all that mattered is our relationship with students.

It's the one thing every educator and student missed as we bunkered at home.

Everything else comes second.

A Note on the Endnotes

Endnotes are usually where the extra commentary by the author and their references are found. However, I was fortunate to have Chris Poulsen read through the first draft of this manuscript and offer his feedback.

While my hope was to make sure I wasn't way off base, what I got was conversation pieces. These pieces eventually formed the basis for our podcast together and with his permission, I asked if I could turn (most) of his comments into endnotes.

Genesis

There was an intent to do a follow-up to Transforming the Heart, but midway through the project, it was set aside. I conducted many interviews with veterans in the field of teaching Religion and I noticed a common trend that warranted a book all on its own.

Successful Religion teachers get that way because of what they do outside the content. The content is important and they all had creative ways of presenting it, but the reason students were on board was for a different reason.

It occurred to me the lessons of that book weren't specific to a Religion class, but to any educator working with young people. I've attempted to name that and talk specifically about it here.

Make no mistake, this is not a "solution" to education.[1]

That doesn't exist.

Rather, it's a way of approaching it that allows a teacher the freedom to try many ideas while enjoying what they do.

Also, in keeping with my philosophy that a book should only be as long as it needs to, I've attempted to do that as well.

Shorter chapters.

Applicable content.

What Master Teachers Know

There's no real secret to teaching, but I'm going to offer one anyway:

Get students on board with you and they will follow you anywhere. [2]

In the countless books, tweets, blog posts and conversations I've had with master teachers, they've all had that one trait in common.

Their approach to the classroom can vary across the pedagogical spectrum, but the core of their method is getting students on board with them. For instance, Jamie Escalante ("Stand and Deliver" and *The Best Teacher in America*) gave daily quizzes, kicked students out with the threat of never being invited back and kept his students strictly in line. Some of his methods were innovative, but students didn't care until they realized he cared about *them and their success.*

And that's the key right there. He established rapport with them.

However, and here's the kicker, it's about *showing, not telling.*

Take, for example, the following two approaches:

"Listen Terrie, I care about your success, but I can only do so much. It's up to you to try harder on the next assignment."

"Here's what we can do, Terrie. I've been tracking your progress this term and noticed a decrease in effort for your last few assignments and I want to reverse that trend. So I'm going to check in with you every day to see where you're at with this latest one and if it's going downhill again, we're going to sit down right away. I'll call your parents and let them know as well."

The second one sounds draining, but it's obvious the teacher is putting more effort into seeing positive results with that student.[3]

In the first few weeks of classes, these teachers know an upfront investment into their students, at the cost of fully fleshed curriculum based lessons, will give them *more time* afterwards. That's not to say no learning is happening, it's just skewed in favour of rapport building.

As my friend Chris would say, "a joyous class can get more done in ten minutes than a miserable one can in ninety."

Does it mean every student will be on board?

No.

Even the most popular teacher celebrities will tell you (if they're honest), one hundred percent enthusiasm never happens.

And that's okay.

I would rather have most students on board all year than fighting to get half of them at the end.

Also, it isn't about being liked. That is *never* the aim. Building rapport is significantly different and demands you still keep your professionalism in tact.

My aunt, a retired teacher who had a reputation for being the greatest teacher any student has had (and also developed curriculum and was way ahead of her time in methodology), offered this piece of advice to me when I started:

"Spend time getting them on board with you. That's it."

I suppose it's the reason two of my best compliments have been the following:

"I've *never* seen a student population attach to someone so fast."

"Vito, you just have to look at a student for ten seconds and you've built rapport with them."[4]

It was something I was doing subconsciously and my students kept telling me how much they loved having me as their teacher. This was humbling because I still have a long way to go in honing my craft and I spend a lot of time learning from others while making mistakes in my own practice. However, students are willing to overlook it and still produce work that showed ample learning.

There are several other factors that contribute to successful teaching, countless really, but it all starts with getting students on board.

In order to do it, one must be willing to teach outside the curriculum.

On the Cult of EduCelebrities

There was a wonderful thread on Twitter about the "EduCelebrities" that dominate the platform. These are educators who have exploded in popularity thanks to their ideas, methodology, or (if you really dig beneath the surface) marketing.

The gist of the thread is their online personas have elevated their egos, and therefore their insecurities, to jerkface jerk status. Not all, of course, but they create a precedent for others to be like them.

I have no doubt there is a genuine care for the craft of teaching and willingness to elevate the practice so that all may benefit, but some honesty is needed.

Where the EduCelebrities are concerned, there is a feeling (whether intentional or not) that if everyone adopted their way of thinking, we will have fixed education. Period.

Yet, we never hear of their struggles, their issues, their failures and heartbreaks. This is a concern to me, especially for those who follow them with blinders on.

It can give a teacher (especially young in their career) a sense that if they're not perfect, with 100% buy-in from their students, they're failures. It's devastating and can lead to burnout quite easily.

It's the responsibility of an educator to keep learning, keep growing and keep adapting... while always keeping in mind this is for the benefit of students and not other educators on social media.

This book presents many seeds to be planted. These are seeds I've gathered from a wide assortment of educators. It's up to you, the gardener, to find out what seeds work best in your garden and to seek out others if what you find isn't here.

Building Rapport the Magician Way

This book highlights the rapport building from a variety of angles as there's no one sure-fire way. Each one is dependent upon the person and what works for them. Some teachers build rapport by getting their students to buy into what they're learning. Others do it through simple gestures, compounded daily.

Each has their own merit.

I spent over ten years as a professional magician, performing to a wide variety of audiences of different ages and demographics. While you would think having a solid repertoire of magic tricks is all that's needed to entertain, it's only the entrance fee. Yes, you need to be really good at your art, but if you want to book shows, you need to get the audience on board with you.

Believe me when I say that if a person doesn't like a magician because of the way they conduct themselves, they won't book them for a show. Even if they're the best at what they do and the audience requests them, the person booking will make any excuse not to bring them in. I've seen it happen.

The seven lessons I learned as a magician have been the perfect carryover to the classroom. Yes, it helps that I actually know magic, but if the students aren't on board with the teacher, magic tricks became a lame gimmick instead of an augmentation to rapport building. These seven lessons are also subtly in place for many other teachers who may not realize they're using the same techniques.

Lesson 1: The Audience Doesn't Care

An audience doesn't care how long you've been practicing, who you studied under or any other resume point that would impress a colleague. They don't want to hear about you.

The difference between an amateur magician and a professional one is the pro centres their show on the audience, not the audience on the magician.

Once the audience realizes the magician is on their side, they will want the magician to succeed. Even if the magician fails one of their tricks, the audience will feel the pain of that failure instead of being callous towards the performer. They want to be on board and are willing to go along with the show instead of passively observing or even heckling it.

Of course, the performance, and the magic, still needs to be good.

There should be evidence of a master at work and someone who has spent time honing their craft. Even a well-liked person cannot hide a pitiful performance beneath their charm. The master magician knows how to build rapport while entertaining, leaning more towards the rapport building at the beginning of the show and building to a stunning climax at the end.

If the balance is right and the magician pays attention to the magic outside the magic, this can be done in any style: comedy, theatrical, strange, street and even silent.

It's the story of magic and the story of the magician.[5]

I can never say I became a master at the craft and I often got the balance wrong on some shows (when you spend too much time rapport building, the audience gets frustrated at the lack of

TEACHING OUTSIDE THE CURRICULUM

magic), but I was always learning and tweaking. Even routines that were solid, original and honed over many years were still subjected to minor tweaks.

Also, it didn't matter how many times I performed an act. No matter how redundant it may be for me, it's the first time for them, or they've booked me again to see it one more time. Even if I was bored of it and wanted to retire it from my show, it was still original to the audience.

Personal accomplishments may have been enough to get people in the door to see a show, but the bragging stops when the show started. At that point, the audience doesn't care anymore. They want to see good magic and they want to feel like part of the show, not just a prop.

***

How often do we make our classes about students?[6]

We can spend time berating our students for being apathetic and not understanding our level of professional judgment, but have we given them a reason to care? Simple gestures go a long way in a classroom and they certainly get noticed by every student.

How fast did you learn their names?

Do you greet them at the door when they come into your room?

Do you wish them a good day when they leave?

Do you take a moment to ask them how things are going in their lives?

If they told you something about their personal life, such as a tournament they're competing in, do you remember to ask them how it went?

Do you treat your lessons with the same enthusiasm every year, or drone through them like a robot?

Do you constantly make the class about you?

These are tough questions and can produce defensive reactions, present company included, but they need to be asked. Students do care if you show them a reason to do so.

Lesson 2: Consider the Needs of Your Audience

The patter used for a children's show should be drastically different than an adult show. Even the routines that are chosen for both shows are chosen with care that will appeal to that particular audience. Dressing up an adult act by adding childish language to it will be lost on children. Going in the opposite direction (dressing up a children's act in adult language) will play very badly.

Master magicians have a pulse on their audience. They know ahead of time what to expect, what people are hoping to see and what the atmosphere will be coming in. If they're doing strolling magic at a restaurant, going from table to table, they know the show is over the moment the food hits regardless of how well it's going.

There's subtleties that need to be considered in each environment and with each audience.[7]

The magician wants to come across as welcoming, not threatening. Body language is incredibly important to building rapport with the audience. Having an open pose is preferable to hands crossed over the chest while waiting for the show to start. While nerves always play a part in every show, it should never be visible. The magician's energy should also match their audience.

Everything from the costume (or outfit), body language and material is carefully considered for each audience as well as the environment the magician will be performing in. When done correctly, the audience will feel like the show was crafted just for them.

***

Do we really consider the needs of each of our classes, and each of our students, and what would work right for them? No two classes are ever the same and even though one lesson/assignment/test worked perfectly for one group, it does not mean it will work for another. I've been caught on this one multiple times.

This would also be a good time to mention a teacher should always avoid current pop culture references in their classes. In fact, I would go as far to get rid of them completely, especially those from past years that are still stuck in current material.

Why?

Students hate it.

It looks like you're trying too hard and unless the teacher is also a performer (or comedian) who studies the art of timing and delivery (although rare, I do know a few), it'll be met with eye rolls.

References from years ago might also go over current student's heads.[8] The teacher has been around much longer than them and can appreciate the endless fads that happen through the years. Students are much younger and only have a memory for the latest.

Don't even try to like their music or call attention to it.

Music is *their* thing and it's personal, just like it was for us. Remember when a teacher tried dropping names of current artists and songs in your classes? It only works if poking fun and leaving yourself open for them to play back at you.

At the same time, the teacher should also be up to date with the interest of their audience. Slow moving movies with heavy

TEACHING OUTSIDE THE CURRICULUM   17

dialogue may have been the norm twenty to thirty years ago, but that won't work today. Snapchat may be the social media home for every teenager today, but the digital age moves fast and they'll be on to something else tomorrow. Take the pulse, but don't make it permanent.

The first time I heard, "My dad listens to Wu-Tang," I knew it was time to stop using it as a reference point.

Lesson 3: You Never Stop Thinking and Practicing

A magician is always thinking about their show, or magic in general.

Everywhere they go, they are constantly ruminating about how the objects around them can be used for magic. It's impossible to listen to music without thinking what magic act would work well with it. If my wife had a dime every time I used the phrase, "this would be great for magic," she could retire as a millionaire now.

You can always tell if a person is a magician based on what they're doing with their hands. If it looks like they're washing their hands in the air while staring off into space, they're actually practicing a move. In their hands is a coin, a ball, a deck of cards, a string, or some kind of object, and they're going through the motions. Sometimes, they may even be holding the object.

Time watching a television show or movie is unconscious practice time. Waiting in line, for the bus or for someone to show up is also ripe for practice. In their heads is the music, or the lines that accompany each movement. Heaven forbid if a eureka moment happens where a synergy of ideas and practicality of "moves" come together in the magician's head. They will run home right away to test it.

At the end of every show, the magician is running through every act and the audience response to each. What worked? What didn't? What can be tweaked? What can be thrown out?

The most important thing a magician really thinks about is how they can make their show uniquely them. Yes, magicians are

TEACHING OUTSIDE THE CURRICULUM

notorious for stealing bits from other people's act, but to copy the script outright comes across as forced. Even the most inattentive audience member can recognize a magician who is not speaking in their own voice.

Everything from the cadence of speech to the way the magician moves is practiced and honed until it feels natural. If I was in conversation with people and (somehow) managed to make them laugh, I would hold on to that line. I would refine it and use it at every opportunity until it made people laugh every single time. Then I would add it to my show.

While this may be a callous representation of what goes on inside a magician's head, especially if you're trying to entertain a conversation with said person, consider what's really happening: they are being extremely observant and self-reflective. Everything is under scrutiny and every detail is reflected upon.

***

How often do we reflect upon our own teaching practice?

We all have bad days and can usually point to the moments where an error happened on our part, but are we thinking about ourselves or our audience? What did we observe about them?

The best advice I received as a student teacher came as an off-handed comment from a teacher mentoring another teacher candidate. Upon asking how this colleague/classmate of mine was doing, he responded with the following:

"Like a new teacher, she is constantly asking how am I doing? What she should start asking is how are *they* doing?"[9]

Are we thinking about how our students are doing? Do our preparations (lessons, assignments, tests) take into careful consideration what we've observed about them? Are we trying to serve them in all we do, or are we out to get them?

We have some pretty unique personalities in every class and while we can categorize them according to personal experience with similar types, have we figured out how to reach them?

Do we look at ourselves honestly and ask how we're growing?

Are we growing at all?

There are a million questions that come with self-reflective and observant behaviour, which is enough to drive any person to back down and retreat to the familiar. However, if we're willing to trudge through the mud, we will slowly be making our way towards much greener pastures.

Lesson 4: Find Your Voice

When you first start as a magician, you tend to follow other magicians patter word-for-word. You don't know any better and the focus is on making sure the magic performs flawlessly as opposed to the experience of the audience. Even if the magician is a silent performer, the beginning magician will follow their movements as precisely as possible.

Over time, you adapt what you're doing and refine the routines until they become your own. Being funny in magic, or at all, is extremely *hard* and the best magicians avoid the overused jokes in their act in favor of joyful moments with audience members. Being serious, or performing at high-octane drama, requires a serious inner belief that what's happening is real.

Audience members intuitively know when a magician is acting out of character. It's the equivalent to an adult using "baby-talk" to someone younger than them rather than using a simplified vocabulary in their regular voice. The magician must figure out the difference between who they want to be and who they actually are, then refine that "character" until it can be no one else. It doesn't have to be unique, just uniquely them.

This is a long process for someone unaccustomed to being an honest performer, but it produces the top magicians in the world. No one else can duplicate the style of David Copperfield, Criss Angel, Penn & Teller, David Blaine, The Amazing Jonathan, etc. because their voice (stage presence) is solidified. Even the local magician with a solid reputation for a certain style of performance cannot be duplicated without the audience calling them out.

When the magician eventually finds their voice, the development of their routines going forward are set. They know how they must work each act to fit their voice and subsequently, their routines become unique variations from the crowd. They also know their voice will not appeal to everyone and they accept they may not be the right fit for some audiences.

However, the audience knows who they are going to get when a magician finds their voice. There are no surprises and this is a true comfort.

***

We all know the use of 'teacher-voice' for the classroom, but how hard have we worked to turn 'teacher-voice' into our voice?

Teacher A and Teacher B both have smoothly run classes with students who are attentive to their every word, even though one is extremely loud (can be heard across the school on another floor) and the other rarely goes above conversational tone. Both work and both are uniquely them.

Do we strive to find the most authentic version of ourselves and deliver it to our students?

Do we fall back on what we assume *should* work based on observations in another classroom?

Do we try too hard to imitate someone else because we're afraid of how students will respond to the real us?

When students begin poking fun at your mannerisms and cadence (not in a mean way, of course), you've found your voice.

When they know who they're going to get from day one to their final day of school, you've found your voice.[10]

Lesson 5: Don't Relate, Connect

"You need to relate to your audience" is actually bad advice.

An audience cannot relate to a person who spends every waking hour thinking about the best way to palm a card. Nor can they relate to someone who is willing to spend three years building and refining a two minute routine. A magician certainly can't relate to an audience who will go home and not completely dissect every minute of their magical performance.

I grew up in a very comfortable middle-class upbringing to two wonderful parents and three incredibly strong sisters. If I'm performing for under-privileged children who may not have a parent and are in survival mode most days in their neighbourhood, how do I relate to that?

Connecting to an audience is far more valuable.

A magician connects to the audience's needs. If they're performing at a wedding, strolling around during cocktail hour to entertain until the festivities begin, they match the mood. They're an extra in the extravagance of the day and keep the dialogue light-hearted and fun. They connect to an audience by keeping the fun going.

On stage, the magician connects to the audience by acknowledging they exist and talking to them rather than at them. They don't insult the intelligence of the audience and volunteers who are brought to the stage are treated with respect, as opposed to being mere props.

The magician treats his audience as sharing in something together. They're connecting to each other over this art called magic and exploring the wonder of it through the act of the magician. Even the magicians with the best technical skill can lull an audience to sleep if they make their show all about them ("Look what I can do"/ "Aren't I great?"/ "You can't catch what I'm doing").

In return, the audience wants the magician to succeed. Their inner dialogue is cheering for every success of the show and they want to do their part to make it a reality. I have seen audience members purposefully lie during the revelation of a trick ("Yep, that's it!") just so the magician wouldn't mess up their show. However, the revelation was supposed to fail in order to procure an even greater revelation. It actually takes coaxing from the magician to convince the audience member it's okay they didn't get it right.[1]

Connecting to an audience is a way of showing respect. Trying too hard to relate can actually be insulting. A magician must carefully thread the needle between the two, but the string is tied on the connection side.

***

Do you know more about your students than their in-class behaviour and marks for their report cards?

If they've been away, do you ask them how they're doing upon their return? If they went on vacation, do you ask them how it went?

If a student fondly speaks about their pet, do you take the time to learn the pet's name and ask how it's doing from time to time?

Do you make it a priority to have one-on-one time, however brief, with each of your students every week?

Do you follow through on what you say you're going to do for students?[11]

Connecting to students is hard because you're an adult figure and (in their minds) have no connection to their world. It takes time and is done in many small gestures, not just a few grand ones. It doesn't mean you stop being an adult figure, or a professional, it means you become more of one that is invested in their success.

Lesson 6: Authenticity

The battle for authenticity is a mammoth subject for the magician to deal with as they solidify their reputation. Are they a serious performer? Are they light-hearted in their approach? Is everything done to music? If so, what kind of music? How do they dress for the stage?

At the heart of all these questions lies an even greater one:

Will the audience see through the magician's act?

David Copperfield redefined magic in the eighties by making it sexy, high performing and to the point. During his run of television specials, he worked himself to exhaustion most nights, sometimes almost collapsing during his shows. His obsession with perfection invites the audience to feel a level of authenticity to everything they are witnessing, even if it's through their television.

I've had the opportunity to see him live three times, but the second one is where I want to hone in. I was sitting in the audience excited to see this show as many years had passed since the first time. However, by the second routine, I could tell something was off.

Way off.

I wasn't the only one who noticed it either. Many in the audience got the sense Copperfield was just running through his script, putting no feeling into anything he was saying. The magic was still on-point, but the authenticity was gone.

What happened?

His dad passed away and the funeral was the day before the show.

Yikes.

Of course his show would be off. Unfortunately, he wasn't the only magician to face those circumstances and every professional knows two things: the show must go on and the audience doesn't care. If it sounds callous, just imagine the reaction if he went on-stage before the show and said, "Sorry if I'm off tonight, but I buried my dad yesterday and still feeling the pain of it."

Any human being would feel the pain of that statement, but an audience would still want their show. To keep it authentic, the magician slips in their shortcomings and bits about their life throughout a show while also reacting in a real way. Their personality matches their practice. Even the silent performer can communicate through their gestures as most communication is, after all, non-verbal.

***

Authenticity is a tough line to tow in a classroom as there is a confusion about the term. What students consider "being real" is a teacher being authentic to who they are and where they stand. It does not mean the teacher acts in a way that is any less professional, nor do they give away every waking detail of their life. [12]

It also means you will need to put yourself out there, which is about as scary as asking someone on a first date. There is a fear of rejection or even a lowering of social status with the class, especially since not every student will like you for... well... you.

I understand it is not your job to be liked and that is not what authenticity means either. Your job will not be appreciated by everyone, even if 99% love what you're doing. There's always going to be the few who hate what you do, no matter how you dress it up.[2]

However, what students will appreciate is the teacher who walked in the door yesterday is the same teacher who walks in the door today. They know who they're getting because you've given them no reason to think otherwise.

It's also admitting your shortcomings and not playing the pretend sage game ("Great question and I'll get back to you tomorrow on that one"). It's also admitting when you were wrong and saying, "I was wrong," rather than, "I apologize." The former goes a lot farther in the eyes of your students who can now appreciate you're human.

Authenticity also means, and this is the tough one, your values are the same in the classroom as they are out of the classroom. In other words, the way you act and carry yourself is consistent. If you think you're good at hiding who you are, just know students have spent every day in their school careers reading the body language of teachers. They will know.

Do you feel you are giving the best representation of yourself to your students every day?

Lesson 7: Be Willing to Stretch

The beginning magician is willing to perform magic just about anywhere, for any audience. It's almost necessary as it arms you with the tools you need to be able to face any situation for future bookings.

Case in point, I spent the first part of my magic career performing at open mic nights, bars and daycare centres who were willing to take a free show. Open mic nights taught me that just because you're on stage, people don't have to pay attention to you. Bars taught me the necessity of having to control your audience members and working at daycares taught me that children are the most brutally honest people on the planet.

Seriously, performing for children is actually the *hardest* of all audiences for magicians.

I had no desire to be a bar performing magician, but I took the gigs to learn from that audience. I've performed for kids in all sorts of venues, each one teaching me a little something about how to handle the environment. My colleagues and I performed for all sorts of clients, each one looking for something a little different.

In every case, we had to stretch to meet a client need.

Ever perform magic for a fundraiser for the blind? That took an incredible amount of creativity to figure out how to make each one of my tricks work, considering magic is a visual medium. That is just one of the many examples.

The result is we all became better magicians at the end of each gig.

***

My biggest attraction to spiritual teaching, and Catholic tradition, is the study of mysticism. It's been an obsession of mine since high school and the contemplative side of religion has always been a special calling. After studying it for twenty years, I've learned one important thing:

Nobody cares.

Despite my best efforts to show the beauty of mystic teachings, the poetry embedded within it and the personal benefits that can be gained through its study, a polite nod is about all I get. That's coming from adults, so you can only imagine the response from students.

Even attempting to build a field trip around contemplative spirituality is a hard sell:

"Who wants to travel to the middle of nowhere and live off the land (no cell reception or wifi of course), spend your days working to sustain the place, pray seven times a day starting at 3:30am, complete silence during meals and after 6:00pm *and then* going to bed at 7:30pm to do it all over again?

Anybody?"

For someone who has spent summers at a monastery, I can tell you it's an incredibly peaceful lifestyle. To be removed from society and have time to truly sort through your thoughts while being in touch with the divine is something that can only be experienced.

Unfortunately, it only appeals to a *tiny* niche of people. While the interest in meditation has been rapidly increasing, people seem enamoured towards the Hindu and Buddhist tradition with its seemingly simple teachings (seemingly because the actual teachings and practice require an intense amount of effort).

TEACHING OUTSIDE THE CURRICULUM 31

This has forced me to stretch my approach towards students. It's not so much what appeals to me, but what appeals to them.

I only dipped my toes into the social justice scene growing up, but it's an incredible starting point for students. They can easily be sold on taking a day to help prepare and serve food in a soup kitchen, or take a week to work with the disenfranchised in another area.

My preferred modus operandi during school was to sit quietly and work independently (I still prefer doing that, but then being able to converse with someone about it after), but that's not all my students. Some of them need to converse and work together and as a teacher, it's tough to let go of control of the room.

Endless research is being done on successful ways of learning and while not a single one of them can claim to be the best option, it's worth giving an honest effort into some of those areas. Where I am in life and where my interests lie cannot meet most students where *they* are at right now. I have to stretch to meet them there.

In our own practice, how hard are we willing to stretch to meet the needs of our students?

How far outside our comfort zone do we travel?

Do we give an honest effort when we do try something new? Or do we try it once and lament it was a failure?

Have we sought the advice of our colleagues, especially the ones we normally wouldn't speak with?

Have we figured out what is worth stretching for and do we know what we need to dig our heels into and stand firm?

We don't always have to stay in areas that we stretch into, but we should be willing to at least see what is there.

Interlude: The Swiss Army Knife vs. The Toolbox

Let's pause for a moment.

I could end the book right here with some sentiment that those seven lessons are all we need to be on our way.

Words of encouragement.

Conclusion.

The End.

However, not everything fits neatly into such compartmentalized analogies.

Teachers are often sold (or seek) the swiss army knife for the classroom. The swiss army knife is the "solution" that will solve all your pedagogical woes, instructional preparation and student engagement. The thinking is usually something like this:

"Yes, every student, class and school is different. This can adapt to *all* of that."

Let me repeat what I said at the onset: there is no "solution" to education.

There is not one system, or idea, that will perfectly capture all of your students.

Instead of swiss army knives, we should be filling our teaching toolboxes. The more we pack into them, the more prepared we are to deal with any situation as it arises.

They require more effort, but they are way more versatile.

Consider the toolbox of the chef. They may not always use garlic in their meals, but on the occasions they do, their toolbox may have a garlic mincer or the knowledge in how to use their chef's knife to mince it. Both will get the job done.

That is what our teaching toolbox should look like.

Unlike a physical toolbox that has limited space, our teaching toolbox expands our entire careers if we're willing to constantly add to it.

The second half of this book are other ideas to consider adding to yours.

Listen and Respond

Listening is a skill that requires an inordinate amount of effort and focus. Hearing someone speak is not the same as listening to what they are saying. We have all been in that conversation where, despite our best efforts, the person we're speaking to does not understand what we're trying to say.

Just ask any couple, ever.

When it comes to listening to students, this is even more crucial. Remember, they're young and all older people just don't understand. To be honest, they're right (to an extent). It's not their fault they grew up in the circumstances they did, but it's our fault for blaming them for it.

To listen to students, a teacher must be willing to stop speaking.

They must also get away from their desk and circulating around the room while students are working. If conversations are happening, just listen to what is being said without jumping in. Some comments to red flag for later:

Frustration with the work
Situations happening at home
Feeling overwhelmed
Feelings of boredom
Situations happening in the school among their peers
No talking at all
Why are these red flags?

Frustration With the Work

The student is not getting it, nor is it clear to them. Even with the numerous tools at our disposal and infinite chasm of the online world to help, something just isn't clicking. Instead of being clear headed about a strategy to get them to understand, the student will throw up their arms and admit defeat.

"I just don't get it."

Then it's time to intervene quietly.

Offer opportunities to sit down and create a strategy for studying. Don't offer a solution right away because that's not what they're asking. The student wants to be able to get this on their own without your help.

Situations at Home

This one should come to no surprise to a teacher in the trenches. If there's a situation at home, a student's mind could be elsewhere the entire day. I use the word 'could' here because sometimes being in school is the distraction needed to forget about what's happening elsewhere.

While it may not be your job to figure out what is happening and how it's affecting their daily life, being on the front line means you are usually the first one who gets to hear about it. However, the next step forward is always tricky because they don't like talking about it, nor are they always willing to accept help if it's offered.

Touch base with them privately and if you suspect it should be dealt with through other resources, let those people know. Understand the reporting laws and policies of the school board in terms of what you are hearing and be completely open about that. Often times we are the first contact as a cry for help.

Feeling Overwhelmed

Although there are plenty of resources in place to teach students strategies about dealing with life's challenges, we don't give them an opportunity to practice any of them. It's usually a sheet with different things to do with the expectation the student will do it next time they're feeling stressed. Don't judge them for not being able to handle it.

Recall the last time you were in a very stressful situation. Did you immediately resort to the tools and actions you've been taught? Unless you've been trained, or practiced many times before, chances are that's not where your mind went.

Pull that student from the classroom and tell them to take a walk and catch their breath. Schedule a meditation with the class for sometime that week. Give them a candy bar from your stash (if you have one). Get them to commit to one action that will help with their feelings in that moment.

Feelings of Boredom

This is a red flag for your current lesson. A student who is bored doesn't see the relevancy of the work they're doing or they may find it too easy. It's not a reflection on you, or even the course, but a sign to revisit what you did that day to see what you can improve.

Boredom doesn't equate with lack of entertainment, either. Edutainment is a popular term and can be an expectation, but press on it too hard and it also becomes boring.

Again, boredom isn't a personal reflection on you as a person or teacher. There will never be one hundred percent buy-in to anything you do (and if there is, and it works year after year with *every* student, please let me know so I can share it with the world as you will have effectively perfected teaching). Take the comment as something to reflect upon and see if there's anything you can do.

Situations Happening with their Peers

If there's heavy drama in the school, the students speaking about it will not be focused on their work. It will look like they're working, but they are merely going through the motions while they try to figure out the grand scheme of what's about to transpire.

There are no secrets between students and there's nothing more than large groups love than gossip. Unfortunately, there's no workaround here as even the best attempts to speak about it, quell the rumours or refocus them will have minor results.

The best recourse is to just listen to what is happening and ask if everyone involved will be safe.

As an example, three of my students were out of focus and looked downtrodden. Normally they were jubilant and the firestarter for getting the class riled up, but not today. Something was wrong and I approached them to ask what was happening, as this posture wasn't the norm for them.

They began to speak about a suspension that happened the other day and the repercussions from it, which they felt were unjust. As I pressed them to continue, they spoke about the climate of the school allowed situations like that to happen. There was a great pain in what they're saying and I promised them the climate of my classroom would be anything what they experience outside of it.

As I walked away, one of them said under his breath,

"At least somebody listened."

No Talking at All

The ideal student? Sits down, head down, doesn't say a word and just focuses on getting their work done. Wouldn't that be nice to have a classroom full of students who are so engaged as this non-talker?

While the instinctive response is to let this student be, the lack of talking isn't always a sign of extreme focus. It may be a mechanism to deal with anxiety, or it could be someone who is socially isolated and may be wrestling with their emotions regarding it.

Never ignore this student. Always make an effort to reach out and see how things are going and find some entrypoint for them to open to you. If you see a book, or a hobby attached to this student, ask them about it. You may be the only person who this student will connect with.[13]

You Can't Fake Authenticity

Have you ever tried imitating a comedian, word for word, as if it was your own act, only to have it fall on complacent stares?

Ever wonder why it failed so miserably?

The simple reason is comedy is excruciatingly tough and comedians use an exorbitant amount of subtle techniques that go unnoticed by non-comedians. Also, it's not your act. It's their act, with their voice and the circumstances of *that* audience at *that* time in *that* place dictated how they told their jokes.[14]

Comedians spend their first few years trying not to fail. Then they spend a lifetime tweaking, writing, rewriting and practicing every bit they do. Jerry Seinfeld and Larry David literally closed the door to the office and spent their entire time just writing material for *Seinfeld*. They ignored calls, meetings and everything else just to focus on writing the best show they could.

Starting to get the picture?

Authenticity is not a formula that can be emulated or applied. It's a living organism with many moving parts that requires your full attention for it to be successful. Although I touched upon it in the last chapter, it warrants another visit in a bit more depth.

The best analogy I can give is a couple who is dating. The most authentic part of the relationship begins when the two begin to see the faults in each other and call them out. This is actually a relief for both because it means they can start being more of who they are without fear of rejection from the other person.

It also means they can take ownership of the relationship, themselves and their responsibilities to each other. Only when that happens does the relationship start to develop depth, where the highs are much higher and the lows are more painful. The two are putting themselves out there for each other.

In being an authentic teacher, it is only you who will be putting everything out there for your students. They will not respond to you unless they see it from you first. Now, if you have no desire to get them to respond, be ready to accept the classroom for what it is and not what it could be.

Let me be clear this does not mean you need to be bleeding your life story for them. Going back to the example of Jaime Escalante, he was incredibly tough with his students. He would constantly kick them out if they weren't willing to keep up.

However, he genuinely wanted his students to hit the highest levels of achievement. Once his students recognized this from him (after leaving the hospital against doctor's orders to go back and teach his class), they were on board with everything he did. They knew his concern for their success was authentic.

Words are important, but actions are loud. Your actions will always dictate whether the words you're saying are true.

TEACHING OUTSIDE THE CURRICULUM

Closing the Door

There's what the curriculum documents mandate you teach and then there's the time you need to close the door and teach off book. The best lessons come from these moments.

What's going on with your students right now?

If you can answer that question, you'll know how to pivot your lessons to play right into their worldview. It isn't a surefire way to get them to open up, but it comes a lot closer than another typical day that ignores their lived reality.

The concern when doing this is threefold: if your lessons keep going off book, you may not cover the curriculum as it was intended. That isn't necessarily a bad thing, especially if you're still managing to teach them the beauty of your subject area in a way that meshes with their worldview.[15]

The second concern is when students catch on and purposefully try to throw you off track to prevent you from doing real work. Veteran teachers usually get a good semblance of when students are attempting to do this and even newer teachers catch on rather quickly.

The third concern is a blindspot. It's when a teacher gets so caught up in what they're saying because they think it's important and what students want to hear, so they keep doing it. Where it gets dangerous is the teacher is deluding themself into thinking they're engaging in discussion, when the reality is much different.

What they're really attempting to do is convince students of their own viewpoint because they feel it's correct.

This is not healthy discussion, nor is it rapport building. All it does is frustrate students to the point where they feel their opinions don't matter or they are not being heard.

Closing the door of your classroom to engage outside the curriculum should be done for the purpose of speaking *and* listening.

***

My student bombed his exam.

While the purpose of this exam did not calculate into his final mark (a checkpoint for the course), he was upset at seeing the results. Trying to find the words to convey his feelings, he vacilitated between "This test doesn't say anything about my intelligence," and "Now I feel bad."

As the bell rang for students to move to their next class, I asked him to stay behind while I closed the door on our discussion. I was honest with him.

"I know you feel bad, but don't think for a second this test has any influence on how I see you as a student. All it tells me is how focused you were for one morning without any consideration for anything else going in your life. I don't look at this as your potential. We still have a whole year ahead of us and I know you're going to do really well in the upcoming months. Are you going to be okay for your next class?"

We sat for a few minutes in discussion and he left telling me he felt better. The shock of the moment had worn off and we did have a great year going forward. My hope was our discussion was a teaching moment for him, but it became a teaching moment for me as well.

I should have had that conversation with all my students prior to the exam.

Connect With Every Student

At least once a week, it should be the teacher's mission to connect with every single student. It doesn't have to be an extensive meeting, but a simple greeting and asking how life is going. If there's an opportunity, ask a few further questions and allow the responses to happen as they will.

This may seem tedious, but there's a lot of downtime this could happen. Before school starts is ideal, as is the time just before class starts. If students are working, especially in groups, there's an opportunity right there to connect as you do your rounds helping students in need.

While this would result in being active in the room instead of trying to get work done at your desk (moments to complete administrative work is priceless to any teacher), the chain effect is outstanding.

It's not a matter of being friends with the students, nor will this result in perfect classroom management. Instead, your students will start to slowly open themselves up to you, trust you and give honest feedback when solicited. They will also take responsibility for their own decisions, even if they willingly avoid the positive ones you want them to make.

Where it gets difficult are the students who, for lack of professional terminology, drive you up the wall. You are their teacher and they are only with you for a short period of time. Separate the behaviour from the task and put extra effort into making sure these students are visited every week as well.

TEACHING OUTSIDE THE CURRICULUM

Students are paying attention to where you spend most of your time. If they see that each of them will get visited, the idea of favouritism loses its ground.[16]

Outside the Classroom Counts

A work/life balance is a careful measure that needs to be measured for a teacher's sanity. However, a teacher's work is their life.

The moment you leave the classroom, you are still a teacher in the eyes of students, parents and the community. While your colleagues, friends and family may know you in a different light, your actions are being weighed alongside what you do in the classroom.

While this may sound daunting, exhausting and the need to claim ignorance may arise, it's an opportunity to reframe this as a positive. The rapport you build inside the classroom bleeds into what you do outside the classroom and *vice versa*. Sometimes, seeing you out of the context of giving lessons, grades and other administrative work moves you closer to the level of "just another human being" in the eyes of the student.

A teacher's favourite, but eye-rolling moment, is always when a student asks, "What do teachers do after school?"[17] or when students are shocked to see their teachers at the movie theatre/local attraction/coffee shop/mall/somewhere they hang out.

Where this becomes imperative is in the hallways of the school. If you spend time building rapport in the classroom and earnestly try to connect with students, then completely ignore them in the hall - they will know you're just an act.[18]

Keep the Professional Lines Clear

As you begin building rapport with students, they will open up to you in ways you never anticipated. This is wonderful for the student who needs somebody to connect with and trust, but it can easily cross a line. It's important to establish that line from the beginning.

One example would be about your duty as a professional to respond to situations where somebody is in danger. I often tell (and repeat) to my students that if I hear they, or somebody they know, is in a position where they could get hurt, I need and *will* report it.[19]

A student who comes forward for the first time does not want to make things worse for themselves and they often feel intervention will do just that. It's usually summarized with something along the lines of, "Please don't tell anyone." It's a catch-22 of them wanting help, but not wanting people to know they asked for help.

While this may sound tough as students who feel you will tell won't come speak with you, they usually do anyway. If they trust you, they'll talk.

The other line that tends to be flirted with are students who want to use you as a conduit to break rules. I've heard of students who asked teachers to borrow their school keys so they could come later that night to setup a prank. The most common of these, however, seem to be students who want a ride home after school for a variety of reasons.[3]

Even if you feel they are the most trustworthy student, keep your professional lines clear on this one. All it takes is one allegation for you to face charges and the end of your career. I've seen it happen.

Building rapport is not building a network of friends. Students befriending you many years down the road is different than the professional relationship you have with them now. Keep the two distinctive.

Stop Taking Yourself So Seriously

As a teacher, you are going to be made fun of by your students. Let me repeat: you *will* be made fun of by your students.[20]

The difference between a teacher who has built rapport and one who has not is the students will do it (in fun) right to your face. If there's no rapport, they will do it callously behind your back.

I'm letting you know right now that you have quirks which students have picked up on. You also have weaknesses they are aware of and habits you might not be aware of in yourself. They're watching your every move, every day, and know you better than you think.[21]

While being careful not to be particularly self-deprecating, I try to point it out before they do. Then I laugh about it.

The flip side to this is something that eventually happens to all teachers: a parent will call to complain about you. It's more likely they will complain directly to you, but it will happen.

However, you would be hard pressed to find a teacher in the field for more than twenty years who hasn't received a complaint. If you do, please send me their contact because I want to know their secret.

Since it's going to happen, do not take it as a personal affront. Hear the complaint for what it is, do your best to deal with it and then move on. To dwell on it is to hamper all the good you are doing.

When Rapport Fails

No matter what you do, how much compassion you show or how much effort you put into reaching every student, there are still going to be those who are not on board with you. These are students who have simply resigned themselves to being antagonistic to you, their peers and education in general.

Continue with what you're doing, but don't burn yourself out. It's usually a circumstance out of place that is preventing any further progress. This could be something simple like time (they need a few years) or more complex like location (physically, emotionally and/or mentally).

Two words of caution.

First, don't confuse these students for your most defiant ones. Yes, sometimes it can be from that batch, but it's usually the defiant ones who turn into your strongest advocates with enough time and care.

Second, don't allow these students to drag you down in a power struggle. They may want to bring you to a lower level just for the satisfaction of knowing they've affected you in some way. When they get the message it's not going to happen, they will begin to target other students.

Take charge and take control. This is still your classroom and you are still the professional.[22]

You Still Need to Teach

Just like the politician who wins an election on charm, then never follows through on a single promise made, you will instantly lose credibility with students if you're not teaching them something.

With the glut of professional resources out there, many free, there's no reason why you shouldn't strive to have an engaging classroom from day one. Students should leave feeling like they've accomplished something and they've been challenged.

For them, the classroom is a place where learning comes alive and all that effort you put into getting them on your side was to show them this fact. In the twenty first century, which we are currently in at the time of this writing, the purpose of education has moved beyond information dumping and the role of the teacher is changing alongside it.

This doesn't excuse a teacher from not taking an active interest in their courses or the subject matter. The passion for education should be prevalent in all you do as students will feed off of it. You are not offering them a disposable commodity, but the potential to be lifelong learners. We can easily take for granted how wonderful it is to have publicly funded education available to every young person in our society.

The style in which you teach should, like the rapport building, still be your own. Whether you're a gold personality-rigidly structured individual or a laid back see-where-things-go person, take ownership of it. You can't be everything for every student, but you can set the expectation for the year and challenge students to meet you there.

How Do I Fit it All In?

With so much to cover, can we really be spending our time outside of the curriculum?

There's a common line you always hear during a professional development session or at the end of a staff meeting when a new initiative is introduced:

"We know you're busy and don't want to add any more to your plate... *but—*"

Or, "We're trying not to interrupt your classes too much... *but—*"

The proverbial *but*.

Every year, it's just one more thing:

One more initiative.

One more task.

One more.

One more.

One more.

It's challenging enough to meet the curriculum requirements without having to think of just one more thing to do in your classroom. And now I've added to that by asking a prioritization of connection over anything else.

There's a great metaphor I heard at a Math conference from David Martin in which he describes rocks, pebbles and sand. His metaphor is actually a visual of what many teachers already do, but just don't tell people.

He suggests to go through the curriculum requirements of a course and label each one either a rock, a pebble or sand.

Rocks are critical areas to cover. A rock is an area that students will need as a foundation for future courses, other courses and/or their own lives.

Pebbles are curriculum points that can be merely touched upon because it will be covered in depth at some other point.

Sand is content that you can easily just slip through your fingers. No one will notice if it isn't covered and no one will really care, either.

For instance, in an English (or Language Arts) class, I would designate a rock as reading and writing in volume.

Focus on your rocks, spend a lesson (two at most) on your pebbles and let the sand slip through your fingers.

Conclusion

This is usually the part of the book where the author sums up their thoughts and gives some kind of encouragement about applying their ideas. However, I've already done that in the text and it might be more useful for a summary.

If I had to do it in one line:

Get students on your side by listening to their needs, responding appropriately and leading them to a place where they can be challenged for something better.[23]

It would also be appropriate to re-iterate not to take it personally when some students just refuse to get on your side. No matter what you do, this may not be the time in their life when they're willing to respond. Keep going, don't burn yourself out and trust when the time comes, they'll appreciate what you were trying.

It may even take twenty years... or longer.

Or, that time may never come.

However, just as we can fixate on the one negative criticism amidst the thousands of positive comments, we can fixate on the few things that went wrong in contrast to the many things that went right.

In other words, stop worrying about the few times when this isn't working in your favour. In many cases, it will only seem that it isn't working.

Students will give you little indication on whether what you're doing is working as its happening, but then surprise you all at once with how much they appreciate it. On top of being a

TEACHING OUTSIDE THE CURRICULUM

tough challenge, the minimal feedback only adds to the difficulty.

Keep going.
Keep striving.
Keep pushing.
Keep challenging.
Keep reaching out.

I'd like to end on story from one of my years in chaplaincy.

I was sitting in my office the second year I was assigned to be chaplain in my school board. The phone rang and it was a student I had many conversations with the year before.

"Hey Vito, how's it going?"

"Loving life!" I replied. "Good to hear from you. How's life after graduation?"

"I'm working on it."

"Are you staying out of trouble?" I asked.

I was being serious with the question. This student missed a year of school after spending time in juvenile detention. He graduated by working overtime the previous year and completing many missed credits. To say he was jaded about life and understood where it could go is underselling his experience.

Our conversations were always open and brutally honest. With a student like this, you don't beat around the bush.

"I am. I'm calling because I have a question."

"Go ahead."

"How do you become a chaplain?"

I was stunned. Based on all the conversations we had, being a chaplain was the least likely avenue I expected this student to go down.

"Well, for starters, you'll have to start going to church."

"I have. I was thinking about what you told me about being in community and started going."

I was not expecting this. This student was serious and the conversation veered towards next steps and what it would take. When I finally asked about the motivation for wanting to go down this field:

"I was thinking of all the conversations we had and how students were always really comfortable talking to you. Thinking about my own life experience, I think it's something that just makes sense for me. I could have a real impact on someone so they won't be as stupid as I was."

All this for being open, honest, challenging and willing to connect with someone who others would brush off.

This is hard work, but it's worth it.

Acknowledgements

It's always a nerve-wracking experience putting out an education book because the field is constantly changing and it's hard not to suffer from imposter syndrome. However, the research, notes and thoughts on this manuscript are a result of the incredible number of wonderful teachers I've had the joy of encountering in my life. They are the ones who paved the way and I give my thanks because I stand on their shoulders.

Even though he's been mentioned several times and appears as a conversation piece in my endnotes, I need to thank Christopher Poulsen. It's through his encouragement that I continue my work and it's from watching him forge ahead on making Religious Education an incredible classroom experience that I know the work is still worth it.

I want to thank all my students I've ever had—I will always hope for the best in each one of you and appreciate what each one of you have taught me.

To my family, especially the many educators within it, you gave me the foundation upon which I stand. Watching you mark student work while we ran around at gatherings as kids showed me that this field is about dedication and a love of what you do.

Writing itself requires sacrifice and you need the support of the loved ones you live with to make it work. As always, thank you to my loving wife who gives me the space, latitude and encouragement needed to see my projects come to a completion.

A big thank you to my team at eVw Press who pull out all the stops to get my work to publication. They say you should never mix friends and business, but it's been all the same for us.

Finally, I want to thank the late Rev. Dr. Ronald Wayne Young. You opened my eyes to this path that I was blindly walking, pushed me forward and set me on course. The many lessons you taught me are finally making sense to me today. Thank you for being my guiding light.

---

[1] *There are instances when the audience member actually forgets and lies to not feel stupid. That's a whole other story, but even that situation can turn into a fruitful one of connection for the magician and audience member.

[2] To see clear a example, do a search for your favourite album, book, television show or movie. I guarantee you will see at least one scathing review.

[3] My professional line on this is pretty clear: *never*.

---

[1] Or....is it?

[2] This is the key to everything.

[3] Thomas À Kempis would say "no one lives in this world free from affliction" (Admonitions for a spiritual life. Ch. 21) and I think we need to choose the afflictions we put on ourselves wisely as this type would lead us and others to Christ

[4] I think one of the key things to honour here to is that it needs to be real. You can put on the act of building rapport with students and at the end of the day take off the teacher costume. But for it to be real it NEEDS to be REAL.

I had a parent once tell me their student came home and say "You know mom, Mr. Poulsen is the real deal.

I think the two go hand in hand.

[5] Curriculum = Expectations

Narrative Theology = The journey we walk with the students.

TEACHING OUTSIDE THE CURRICULUM

Become a character in their story that they want to keep alive.

Help them to realize they are the main character in their story. (And that it's the most important story they will ever have)

[6] How many teachers forget that our students and their parents are, in fact, our bosses paying our salaries....why the hell would it not be about them?

It's easy to become arrogant in this profession. It's easy to become high and mighty. It's easy to become an asshole.

[7] This mean KNOW YOUR STUDENTS. Know their issues. If you don't give a damn about the person you won't be able to fake giving a damn about the student.

[8] I know of a teacher who would use The Simpsons references constantly and none of the students would ever get the reference. The end result was that both parties disengaged from each other. The students obviously thought the teacher was lame (and rightly so). But the teacher was so appalled at the lack of understanding the kids had of the perennial television show that he withdrew from them as people.

[9] I think they two mirror each other. We also need to have an understanding that 8-3pm is teacher time and what cost are we putting on that time? Is 8-3pm worth the new teacher no social life, constant stress, etc.? Is 8-3pm worth the fight with your wife and the frustration at your children? How can we turn 8-3pm into something that fills us up to be better for the people that matter most?

[10] This whole section is another massive challenge. What we call "Finding Your Voice" as a teacher could be worded in a

more terrifying way: "How much of yourself are you willing to put into your teaching?"

This is an absolutely terrifying concept. Do students know the character Mr. Michienzi? Or do they know Vito Michienzi with all of his wonderful things, flaws, history, hopes, dreams, and shortcomings? It ties back to being the real deal.

[11] Summed up: Do you pretend to care OR do you actually care about them?

[12] One might say authenticity often shows itself in the walls the teacher builds and the lines they draw in the sand.

I give a whole 30 minute lesson on how to pronounce my name...because it's important. They end up saying my name right, but more importantly understanding the value I place on having "a good name" and valuing that.

[13] Silence and unquestioning obedience are often the symptoms of larger issues. Kids aren't good at masking their hurts.

[14] This drudges up a major foundational problem associated with Religious Education departments that may be unfixable:

-IT DOESN'T MATTER IF YOU LOVE JESUS

-IT DOESN'T MATTER IF YOU GO TO CHURCH EVERY SUNDAY

-If you aren't a trained theologian who isn't afraid to go outside the church and wrestle with the tough issues and not care what side you land on you will be nothing more than a mouthpiece of indoctrination.

Our teachers need to be theologians.

[15] And truly...I think that in our off book time we cover more curriculum then we really think. RE curriculums are flimsy

TEACHING OUTSIDE THE CURRICULUM

at best and the knowledge component is nothing that a "hey siri" can't give us.

[16] You are really speaking here of the value of going off task. It's crucial. I think you need to go further and overtly say it though: Take kids off task to be human with them. Whether it's the task of getting to class in the morning, or when they are supposed to be working on something in your class, or eating their lunch. The value of taking them off task to be human with them will make those connections. You know it has worked when you have a moment and then they tell you "I've got to get back to work now" with a smile!

[17] The best teachers have the guts to say "Well Johnny, I'm drinking my face off this weekend...and it's because of your class."

[18] The beautiful dichotomy you have been weaving goes full circle in this line. This is the single most powerful line in this document.

Magic, Entertainment, Etc... it IS an act.
Teaching authentically CAN'T BE.
This is more powerful than you know!

[19] Worth mentioning: Our hands our tied. Policy and Law around reporting makes our decisions for this.

But being open about it is the authentic choice we need to make.

[20] And...if you're the real deal....you'll have the confidence to give it right back to them!

[21] For years the going thing about Mr. Poulsen is that they think I'm always drunk because of how I have developed my

meticulously planned lessons and speeches to sound like stream of consciousness.

[22] The key to this is to think of the breakup analogy.

When we go through a breakup that wasn't our choice we often pine and cry over the person who broke up with us. But that's blind behaviour.

Why in the hell do we grieve over the people who don't want us in their lives? Why do we give so much our most valuable resource (time) to them.

Don't ignore, dislike, write off, or hate the students who aren't on board with you. Always go above and beyond for them in the capacity of teacher. But let them make the choice not to connect and don't let it become your mission to connect. It's ridiculous to see a class go by the wayside because a teacher needs to connect with someone who doesn't want to do the same.

I have a million examples of this we can talk about. It's not callous...it's objective truth: Don't waste everyone's time.

[23] My one line summary: If you want real outcomes—be the real deal.

About the Author

Vito Michienzi is the author of several books including *Transforming the Heart: Teaching High School Religion*, *We Are All Broken*, *Less but More* and several works of fiction. In addition to being a writer, he also teaches high school Religion and is an avid reader.

He lives in Ottawa, Ontario with his wife and children.

Read more at www.vitomichienzi.com.

www.ingramcontent.com/pod-product-compliance
Lightning Source LLC
Chambersburg PA
CBHW031417040426
42444CB00005B/606